A-Z Of Cafe Culture: A Millennial's

Reflection on Modern Cafe Culture

Alexander Paul Burton

A-Z Of Cafe Culture: A Millennial's Reflection on Modern Cafe Culture

Alexander Paul Burton

Contents

If Timmies Could Write Coherent Poetry, it Would Be Actually Quite Good.

There's a peculiar duality to my sense of self — a low hum, somewhere between espresso shot and black tea. Born of a Canadian father yet raised squarely in the British Isles, I've always found myself hovering between worlds. Identity, belonging, and the way place shapes perspective are more than passing fascinations. They're quiet fixations, often spilling out into the way I observe space — especially the kind of space we barely think about. Cafés. Caffs. Coffee shops.

Whatever your poison. This book — *A–Z Of Cafe Culture: A Millennial's Reflection on Modern Cafe Culture* — grew out of those spaces. It is an attempt to chronicle, to muse upon, and perhaps to understand these unique public parlours that punctuate our lives.

A Sip Through Time: A Brief History of Cafes

The concept of a public space for refreshment and socialising isn't new, though the coffee itself took its time to arrive on many shores. While not "cafés" in the modern sense, ancient Romans had their *thermopolia*, bustling street-front counters providing hot food and drinks, and *popinae*, simpler places for wine and social interaction, serving as early precursors to public gathering spots. Throughout the Medieval period in Europe, taverns and alehouses were the primary hubs, offering alcoholic sustenance and a place for communal life, long before caffeine entered the scene.

The true story of the café, however, begins in Africa, specifically in the highlands of Ethiopia, the legendary birthplace of the coffee bean. From there, coffee cultivation and consumption spread to the Arabian Peninsula.

By the 15th and 16th centuries, the Middle East was home to the first recognisable coffee houses, or *qahveh khaneh*. In cities like Mecca, Cairo, Damascus, and Constantinople (modern-day Istanbul), these establishments became vibrant centres of social, intellectual, and even political life. Patrons played chess, exchanged news, listened to

7

storytellers, and discussed affairs of the day, making them crucial nodes of communication and culture.

Europe's introduction to coffee was more gradual, with the beverage arriving via Venetian trade routes in the early 17th century. The first European coffee house is believed to have opened in Venice around 1645. The idea quickly spread. In 17th and 18th century London, they blossomed as "penny universities" — spaces where, for the price of a coffee, you could access information, hear gossip, debate, and start companies. Lloyd's of London, the famous insurance market, began at one such establishment. Ideas swirled faster than cream in a long-black.

Paris, too, embraced the café with fervour, its establishments becoming haunts for Enlightenment thinkers, artists, and revolutionaries. Vienna, legend has it, saw its first coffee houses after the Battle of Vienna in 1683, using captured Ottoman coffee beans. Of course, these early European places often excluded women and many others — a reminder that even the most "liberated" third spaces have historically had gatekeepers.

Later, in Britain, the distinctly unpretentious "caff" took over — greasy, comforting, and vital. Egg, chips, tea, repeat. No laptops, no latte art. Just formica tables and regulars with names like Dave. That culture still lingers in some corners, a testament to the enduring need for simple, accessible community spaces.

The Modern Brew: Cafe Culture Today

Now, the traditional caff often sits cheek-to-cheek with minimalist espresso bars serving ethically sourced beans and beetroot lattes. The aesthetic has changed, often dramatically. The clientele too, reflecting shifts in work, leisure, and social norms. But the fundamental function? Not so much. Cafés are where we go to be visible, but not too visible. Where we can be alone but feel less alone. They've become vital "third places" — a term coined by sociologist Ray Oldenburg — public but personal, social but not demanding. They're neither home nor work, and they're more essential than ever in a world that often flattens both into the same four walls and a webcam.

Post-COVID, this only intensified. Our homes became everything: offices, gyms, classrooms, sanctuaries, prisons. And when the world reopened just a crack, cafés took on a new meaning.

For freelancers, writers, Zoom-fatigued office workers, they were a lifeline — a place to reset. The act of "working in public" became more than aesthetic. It became survival. Not just for the customers but, in many cases, for the cafés too.

But we can't talk about café culture without talking about class. Not everyone can sit in a coffee shop all day working on a MacBook. That privilege belongs mostly to information workers — writers, designers, digital consultants, people like me. Meanwhile, the baristas, the delivery drivers, the people cleaning tables and changing bins? Their labour doesn't get remote options.

And yet, paradoxically, remote work — and the café culture that supports it — has also widened access in other ways. For people with disabilities, or caregivers, or those outside of city centres, it offers flexibility that office culture never did.

There's a tension here. Café culture is both liberating and exclusionary. A site of possibility and inequity. A good flat white doesn't erase that.

As a gay man, I'm also acutely aware of the atmospheres I step into. Not every café is friendly. But many independent spots — especially in urban centres — have become de facto queer spaces. Not official. Not rainbow-flagged. But still safe-feeling. Art on the walls, pronouns on badges, indie playlists that aren't just Spotify's "Coffeehouse Chill." These details matter profoundly, signalling welcome beyond the mere transaction.

My Perch and Philosophy: An Observer's Notes

This book grew out of watching people and being watched. Out of noticing that cafés aren't just where we escape to. They're where we perform. Whether you're perched beside a sad-looking succulent in a Balzac's with a flat white and a word doc, or taking someone's oat milk order for the seventh time that hour, the café is a shared stage. And like all stages, it comes with drama, repetition, and those long, lingering in-between moments — resignation, exhaustion, beauty. Sometimes, it's hard to tell the staff and the customers apart in terms of who looks more overworked.

There's this strange intimacy to the space, but it's also anonymous. I've worked in cafés. I've watched people in cafés. And nine times out of ten, we're all too tired to truly care. The politeness is real, sure, but also mechanical.

And yet... beneath that, there's a shared ennui. A quiet understanding. The kind that only exists when people are shoulder to shoulder, strangers with matching eye bags and a mutual dependency on caffeine and Wi-Fi.

Writers and baristas, oddly enough, aren't that different. Both begin their shift with a sense of unknown. A barista opens up shop and doesn't know if the place will be dead quiet or full of toddlers and tech bros by 9am. A writer stares at a blank page and has no idea what mess is about to spill out.

The latte orders and the metaphors arrive all at once. You serve what you can. The page, like the espresso machine, demands something of you. It's a ritual, even if you're faking it. And on some days, even faking it feels like too much.

Of course, most modern discourse seems obsessed with the Cost of Living Crisis (is it still a crisis if it's been literally my entire adult life...?). It's there, subtle and smug, in every overpriced croissant and the unnerving $7 latte. And don't get me started on tipping — a thing I have now internalised as a moral duty, thanks to North American guilt structures.

Still, even morality has a price. So let's talk value — or more precisely, what we get for the price we pay. Sometimes, the only sane thing left to do is lean into the madness. My best advice? Maximise. Make full and proper use of the free milk, the free soy milk, the free water. (Read: hoard.) Consider it a philosophical exercise. Not practical advice, but an invitation to reflect on the slippery nature of "value added" — and on the minor, beautiful fraud of quietly living better within the cracks of late-stage capitalism.

Wittgenstein might call it a language game; Hume would ask whether the benefit was real or perceived. Descartes would deny the milk even existed, while Russell might simply sip it and say nothing at all.

I used to be precious about my writing desk. It's an antique — passed down from my boyfriend's family. Gorgeous, old, impossible to clean. Too many muffins, too many late-night crumpets, and more than one abandoned Burger King wrapper. I keep promising to take care of it, but the truth is, I find more creative clarity in a café than I ever have hunched over that crumb graveyard. Thank you, Dineen Coffee. Thank you, Balzac's. I owe at least four poems and a full chapter to your wall outlets and indifferent indie playlists.

There's a freedom in cafés — a kind of borrowed clarity. You walk in, pick a corner, and become someone slightly better than the you who forgot to wipe down your kitchen table.

You can create a temporary office, a performance space, a micro-kingdom. Alone, together. Everyone else is doing it too.

Sometimes, I eavesdrop. Not out of nosiness — well, not just — but because café conversations are windows into the soul of a place. People break up over croissants. They conduct job interviews between bites of banana bread. I once heard a woman pitch a vegan murder mystery podcast to what I assume was a bored man named Brian. He asked no follow-up questions. She powered through the rest of it.

These moments — brief, absurd, touching — are the caffeine that keeps my writing alive. Cafés are one of the last places where real, unfiltered life unfolds without rehearsal. You don't get that in a coworking space. You don't get that in a Teams meeting. You get it at the sticky table near the bin with bad lighting and the best energy in the room.

Cafés, like people, contain contradictions. They're loud but contemplative. Impersonal but familiar. Rushed but timeless. And that's what I find endlessly fascinating. They're the kind of place where everything — work, life, identity — quietly converges under the hiss of a milk steamer. No declarations.

No grand philosophy.

Just the slow drip of collective existence.

And maybe a crumpet.

Anonymity

Grace, that presence holds aloft,
a fleeting thought - pensive, soft.
A theory of spaces, place to grow,
to write and think, thoughts to sow.

Liquid sipped, a coffee brewed,
save your funds, avoid the food.
For coffee black, tea or bevvie,
a place to write, to feel less heavy.

The writer's haunt is a new home,
a hook, an anchor, free from roam.
So merry dance your thoughts and scribe,
create, explore that cafe vibe.

Black Coffee

It's cheating, I know
but oft required,
for caffeine is your friend.

In harmony with thrift, don't blow,
oft always required,
black no choice, my favourite blend.

The Hack of Hacks,
two dollars more,
gives time to write, to keep it black

Barrista busy, over tired,
respects the choice a writer makes,
complex drink... a bleak mistake.

Comfort

Home beckons, a heartfelt lie,
for third-space comfort doth out-cry.

A time to pause, reflect and stay,
soft plush place, posterior lays.

Corner chair, its wooden slats,
don't sit there: comfort trap.

For cafe sofa is in need,
a writer's place, a trusty steed.

Desk

It's clear to see, an office not,
a single double espresso shot.
Place oft an afterthought,
where coffee flows and thoughts are brought.

More often calm, but busy gets,
an office space for you to set.
Temporary, it is so,
transient this creative flow.

So anchor set, a brief respite,
for writer's block willn't bite.
Golden liquid in a cuppa,
desk with crumbs, remains of supper.

Explain Ennui

Shared space, fractured thought,
a different life, a coffee bought.
Intimate is this space we know,
different feelings in us grow.

Paths tread, travail dread,
a busy queue, energy spread.
For time is oft a currency,
come and go, but not all free.

For though this space is ours to share,
mine reflects, a time to stare.
But that connection, in our paths tread,
to start the day, or page, in dread.

Intimate I know this space,
if not frequented, often placed.
Your career path leads beyond,
to leave this post, and not respond.

Free Will

Freedom square, or circle round
the soft lacquer, steel found.
For your space freely do you use,
a coffee menu: Browse! Peruse!

Space creates, that miniature world,
the mind catalyst, a vision bold.
And though that long time consumes,
those dulcet, modern, lo-fi tunes.

Hip or square it matters not,
for freedom in a coffee shop,
is hence the maker by design,
take free milk, extend your time.

Gush

Early wake up, diminish will,
a liquid shot, that wake-up 'pill'.
The pen confides in paper blank,
that solace, in your mind's word-bank.

For table is a catalyst,
the pen, paper, coffee: a threesome tryst.
The narrow chance that they all meet,
to smudge the coffee with the ink.

But creatives in us all write,
doth caffeine, pen and coffee bite.
Creative flow, the flame ignites,
a solace feeling, end in sight.

For writer's block it is no friend,
when coffee lubricates, thoughts send.
Still we speed, that golden cup -
Catalyst - writers' level-up.

Heuristics

Often an awkward term,
these less used words are held esteemed.

Reality is a different game,
shorter words can mean the same.

Oft refused for sale of breadth,
the choice to use comfort bereft.

Third space needs not words so long,
for writer's block needs no song.

The simple meaning of the word,
this third space for ideas Heard.

So plan away and think out loud,
Heuristics (planning), to lift that shroud

—

Investigate

Oft I find, I found that peace,
present, past and times understood
to free the soul and travel would
spend time, cafe a lease.

For though we stay not long,
a timeless entry, space untold
to watch the world, to watch unfold
a quiet gesture, not a song.

Historic feed of social news,
unfolding status people told
stories mixed, stories unfold,
lloyds of London, business brews.

Laptop layover in our time,
drinks aplenty, options more
things have changed, four score four,
neither clocks in modern chime.

Juxataposition

Find it proud, not so loud
a cry for wallet's pain.
For poet's feeling, is a bane
to call hypocrisy out by name.

Exchange of breath, a hollow chant
for 'twixt thy jangle, coffee's made.
A hymn unwritten, often bade,
call out capitalism, be un-made.

The shallow wish, upon the breath,
the students' learning, naive at best.
For rhyme's sake just leave it be,
to be productive, coffee need.

Sanctimonious: the highest high
a joyful intellectual's outcry.
We know the price, one small cup,
to fight the 'system', shallow try.

Kindness

Passive thoughts, and kindness lies,
behind the tired, caffeine eyes.
A thought provokes sudden, stark.
Privilege, the space shows spark.

Rushed and pushed, a careful dance,
of talk, prattle, careful stance.
Menu long, why so hard?
Keep it simple, speed up tard.

Your game is short a brief respite,
chance encounter, do not bite.
For busy gets, and time is scarce,
ten dollar coffee millionaire.

So tread light, and understand,
to consider that upper hand.
Be a guest, stay a while,
kindness classy, stay in style.

Locations

It's a strange thing, to travel broad,
writer's pen that trusty sword.
Consistent though the drip doth taste,
china, paper, poured in haste.

Matters not and oft is asked,
of Bard, the writing tasked.
Eclectic mix of spots we seek,
avoid it well, that bleak.

Busy some, and quiet not,
of comfy cozy coffee spot.
And in the end of matters little,
To end the page, still committal.

Mundane

The tides are set but not for you,
a word, a mot, creative stew.
Blessed we are, in our lot.

Bentham, Mill - that blessed group,
hold in esteem the writer's stoop.
Space best used in righteous taste.

'Twixt the walls of plaster plain,
the boredom, avoid writer's refrain.
Outcomes wide, democracy of beverages.

Notepad Graveyard

Scions in their bound delight,
oft unused in their state,
for well-intentioned we may be,
pages never see the light.

Writer's book, in unbound thought
at end are full indeed,
and even when those words outspill
uncommon in this cohort.

Out there lives a graveyard still,
mournful aggregate of intention:
well-meant writer, would-be book,
meaningless and empty thrill.

Obscurity

The Library of Alexandria lost,
meticulous its ancient Provost.

Words and books, their many forms:
carved and burnt in world's storms.

Space was full, lover's delight,
Rome Ancient would act contrite.

To know that modern coffee shop,
antithesis for academia slop.

Commercial yes and bitter black,
new ideas form and crack.

Though not one purpose we have here,
obscurity these people queer.

Many forms transactions stew,
Work. Write. Create anew.

Paper

Oft used trope that quiet refrain:
"the pen is mightier than the sword."
Question remains, a modern twist,
that laptop in our cafe bliss.

Tool of study, work or rite.
A modern tool, to many blight.
Question remains a newer trope:
"what creativity can blank screen evoke?"

The silence space doth often see,
The bleed of burn, creativity.
Question remains, I do berate:
"The loss of thought and pen? I hate."

Montblanc, Faber, or LAMY new,
And paper bourne of pumped stew.
Question remains, 'fore ink runs dry:
"Laptops write not words, why try?"

For paper clean, tabula rasa,
British voice: a pen writes 'fastah'.
Question remains, a timeless trope:
"Will thee use pen and ink? I hope!"

Queers & Cheers

Unfriendly glare, a worried stare,
a friendly face... spot them not.
Welcome here? I know this not.
It stains my soul, creative blot.

A modern twist, perhaps of fate,
archaic, medieval, and full of hate.
Welcome here? Where could I go?
New space, a queer can grow.

Though gender, sex a shop has not,
people's hatred doth not stop.
But welcome in a place anew?
Queer space, built to grow for you.

Worry not, Toronto's boon,
Acceptance, being, be a bloom.
Yes to welcome - need not ask!
Stick to writing, stay your task.

R

Reflect

Oft required, buy you cannot,
the drop, the flow,
the word,
the mot.

Word's a hurry, hence do not fear,
the stay, this calm,
creative,
steer.

Sit and ponder, craft unwind,
pen to paper,
laptop,
kind.

S

Sorting Thoughts

Wittgenstein was clever so,
language games, neurons shew.
His haste for words and rationale,
to us poets, seems banal.

Chaos mind, undoubtedly so,
to me a critic, real-life blow.
For I am messy, this is real,
Logical Positivism, not ideal.

Cafe to creatives are,
a place to stretch where words do stew.
Ideals (bilds), to thinker old,
cafe helps my stories unfold.

Embrace the warmth, a seat upright,
pen to paper, tugging tight.
German man, in tweed suit:
not academic, my pursuit

Third-space

Einstein in his witty mind,
joked of God, that he's not blind.
That dice was not a game He knew,
God plays not with chance it's true.

For us mere mortals, earthly bound,
the mustard seed of truth is found.
Ideas born from chance in us,
sse Third Space, and mind you trust.

Heaven's jealous of Human Soul,
for chance is best, un-wind, un-tell.
Observe and soak up world renewed,
the soul needs chance, feed it food.

Unphysical, is truly a word,
But now you've read it, now it's heard.
For Heaven has no coffee stores,
No observe, no view: it bores.

Understated

Talking is my favourite game,
but unassuming is not same.
Fog-horn though I often am,
cafe silence helpeth to plan.

A quiet space to sit and state,
to open mouth not, no care.
Mysterious sitting, ponder so,
I sit in silence, sit and grow.

Vin

At fault sometimes, cultured not,
to venture past intellectual's rot.
Stagnate, expire and hair let down.
middled-aged lady, beset with frown.

Me too, at fault it would seem,
Composed poetic, curated scene.
Oft I wonder, line by line,
the need to sit at lunch with wine.

In Vino Veritas, philosopher bleateth,
To live your life and soul depleteth.
To act, charade, and play the part,
Versailles' mind in our Art.

Mind's folly, to this trend,
as writers boredom be thine end.
Leave the coffee, take a rest,
wine in hand: be you blessed.

Washroom: Where

Pandora's box, it is to ask,
For washroom, restroom, bathroom task,
location not the only fault,
language, accent, 'tis a jolt.

For in mid-west or UK shores,
washroom not a word, assured.
For different words and key codes need,
to unlock bathroom, haste the speed.

But keycode, key or fob you'll get,
a private room, not locked still yet.
But button green or red doth show,
confusing yes, scared to know.

If unsure, just don't ask.
Act in haste, and do your task.
For private this is, and harder still,
damn tricky, not a thrill.

Xpresso Espresso

Conundrum born, continent divide,
or intellectual parasite.
Or mistake Human, not unmade,
to mistake letter, wrong the trade.

To Gallic mind, or Latin langue,
the word with X is pure wrong.
Turtle Island, or lazy mind,
to use 'expresso': culture blind.

So quandary is, remember so:
heed the words before you go.
To order coffee, tiny cup,
pronounce with S. No hiccup.

Y Cr8?

Pen to paper, mind ablaze,
the unsung hero burning haze.
And in this moment we confide,
in private naissance, purely pride.

Repose quiet, silent state,
let the poetry elate.
For 'twixt the algorithm's stare,
and numbers on screen's glare.

Matters not, numeric will,
qualities digital will instill.
A mind of fracture, thought unwind,
creative, parsed and in a bind.

But mind aloof, the pen it sets,
to paper, screen and still begets.
Addictive some would call,
the make, the send, the play, the fall.

Zed or Zee

Zed or Zee, a Canuck's dream,
Brit or Yank: choose a team.

A quandary quiet, need to choose,
in a Brit, it draws the blues.

Grammar correct, COlonial not,
to choose a letter, intellectual's rot.

It's just plain simple, confusing yes,
when words' plethora in us blessed.

Purely Zee, 'gainst national pride,
American Exceptionalism, find it snide.

Brit of Canuck, slightly same,
we, a family, not just in name.

So Zed it is, I know it's old,
Canadian Pride: history bold.

The Last Drip: On Knowing and Belonging in the Cafe's Quiet Hum

And just like that, here we are, at the quiet closing of this alphabetical ramble through the labyrinthine world of café culture.

It doesn't quite feel like an ending... more like the gentle, persistent drip of a coffee maker, leaving a lingering essence and a few dregs here and there. This journey, from A to Z, has been my humble attempt to hold a mirror up to those strange, wonderful public parlours that punctuate our lives – those unassuming stages where the messy, beautiful drama of being human quietly unfolds.

The Quiet Wisdom of the Unseen

Our travels in this book included with the heavy shadow of the Library of Alexandria, that wondrous monument to human knowledge, now lost to the storms of history.

Yet, traversing the letters from Anonymity through to Zed or Zee, a different kind of repository has come into focus. Not one of scrolls and ancient texts, but of quiet hums and clattering saucers. It's a striking thought, truly, that these humble, often overlooked cafés now contain a knowledge capacity, through the simple act of connection and digital access, which probably surpasses that ancient marvel. A personal Library of Alexandria in every pocket, at every single table.

This paradox, a peculiar duality of the grand and the mundane, the weight of history meeting the transient moment, has been the constant, low hum beneath every observation.

It's the liminality of these spaces that resonates deepest with me, as someone who has always felt poised between worlds. Reflecting on Rome's ancient *thermopolia*, or the vibrant intellectual life of the Middle East's *qahveh khaneh*, and even London's industrious "penny universities," it becomes clear that the café's purpose is not merely modern invention.

It is an echo, a continuous thread of human need for connection, refreshment, and the unspooling of ideas. The aesthetic shifts, certainly, from greasy "caffs" to minimalist espresso bars, but the core function endures. They remain vital "third places," spaces for quiet presence, for belonging, even when alone. In the aftermath of the pandemic, their essential role solidified further; working in public ceased being a mere choice and became a quiet act of survival.

The Philosophy of the Daily Brew

In pondering the inherent class dynamics of café life, the observation is not one of judgement, but of nuanced understanding. The privilege of lingering over a MacBook, while acknowledged, only heightens the appreciation for the unsung efforts of those whose labour keeps the wheels turning – the baristas and staff who lend these spaces their patience and good humour.

It is a subtle recognition of a shared dependence, a quiet nod to the fact that even amidst potential inequity, there's a collective human experience at play.

These independent cafés, particularly within urban centres, often quietly become more than just coffee shops. For many, including myself, they evolve into unofficial safe spaces, especially for queer individuals.

It's never about overt declarations; rather, it's the subtle cues—the art, the pronouns, the thoughtfully curated playlists—that weave a tapestry of welcome. These details, perhaps "obscure" to some, signal a profound sense of belonging that transcends simple transaction.

My philosophy has truly brewed from simply watching, and being watched, in these environments.

The café, in essence, is an unrehearsed stage.

Here, life unfolds in brief, absurd, touching moments—a breakup over croissants, a job interview amidst banana bread, a vegan murder mystery podcast pitch overheard. These are the spontaneous details, the raw, unfiltered moments that fuel the creative spirit. There's a strange intimacy to this anonymity, a quiet understanding amongst strangers.

Writers and baristas, sharing the unpredictable nature of their days, find a ritual in their work, a shared ennui that only those shoulder-to-shoulder, dependent on caffeine and Wi-Fi, can truly comprehend.

And yes, the Cost of Living Crisis casts its long shadow, felt in every unnerving ten-dollar latte.

But even here, a subtle philosophical exercise presents itself: the humble maximizing of free milk or water. It's a quiet rebellion, a minor, beautiful fraud within late-stage capitalism. The thoughts of Wittgenstein on language games, Hume on perception, Descartes on reality, or Russell's quiet observation, all feel oddly at home here. The café, truly, becomes a more fertile ground than any crumb-laden home desk.

A sincere thank you, then, to places like Dineen Coffee, Balzac's, Dark Horse Espresso Bar, and Goldstruck Coffee. Their wall outlets and indie playlists have sparked countless chapters and poems. There's a borrowed clarity in these places, a gentle nudge to become a slightly better version of yourself, whatever that really means.

The Unspooling Threads of Purpose

As we draw towards the last drip, the ultimate takeaway from this A-Z is perhaps less about definitive answers and more about the enduring value of these paradoxical spaces.

They are not merely venues for transactions, but incubators for thought, connection, and creation. They remind us that grace can hold aloft in the most unassuming moments, and that even a black coffee can buy precious time to write. They embody the fluid nature of a temporary office, a desk where creative flow, however transient, can be potent. The shared ennui of a busy day, the quiet rebellion of free will exercised through prolonged visits – these are the threads that weave through the café experience.

The café as a catalyst for creative gush, where caffeine and words bite, is a potent image. It is where heuristics can simplify planning, where ideas can truly be heard.

It is a place to investigate the historical echoes of social news, to observe the world unfold, a timeless entry. Here, the juxtaposition of intellectual pursuits against commercial backdrop becomes clear, but so too does the opportunity for a quiet, personal defiance.

These spaces foster kindness, remind us of our guest status, and offer consistent comfort across different locations.

The mundane, in the right light, inspires a creative stew, a democracy of beverages leading to wide outcomes. Even the presence of a notepad graveyard serves as a quiet call to fulfill unused intentions. And in their very obscurity, these cafés somehow *queer* the space, making it a fertile ground where new ideas form and crack, where we truly Work. Write. Create anew.

The ongoing dance between paper and pen versus the laptop in our café bliss, or the crucial quest for safe spaces for queer folks, all find a poignant home here.

So, in these quiet moments, reflecting upon the drip, the flow, the word, the mot that unwind and steer a person's creativity, a profound truth emerges. Engaging with thoughts, perhaps like Wittgenstein, even if my own mind is chaotic, reveals how the café helps stories unfold. It's a third-space in which creativity can flourish and ideas can be nurtured to their maturity.

There's an understated quiet that allows a person to think and grow, despite your own louder tendencies. And yes, sometimes, I might yield to the temptation of lunchtime vin and, in doing so, discover different forms of inspiration when coffee wasn't going to do the job.

This whole book is, I guess, just a testament to the simple, yet profound, fact that creativity, connection, and really good observation don't need grand stages or those long-lost ancient libraries.

They just need a space, a moment, and maybe a perfectly brewed cup of coffee.

So, the next time you step into a café, just take a second. Really look. Listen.

And maybe, just maybe, quietly create anew. The threads of culture, history, and your own unique purpose are unspooling all around you.

It's time to join the quiet rebellion.

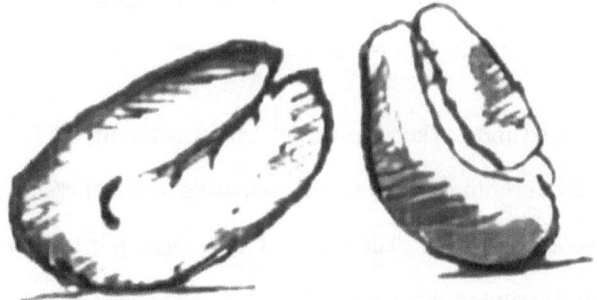

About the Author

Alexander Paul Burton is a writer and composer based in Toronto. Born in Britain and raised across the hills, marshes, and towns of Somerset Cornwall and London, he grew up with a deep love for language, memory, and landscape. His stories often explore the quiet spaces between what is remembered and what is lost—*vethir anneth*, the unspoken truths that live in silence.

He has lived and worked throughout the West Country & London and now calls Toronto, Canada home. Alongside writing fiction, he writes and records music in Toronto and has spent much of his career working in communications and marketing for nonprofits and public sector organisations.

His work is shaped by a belief in the power of storytelling to hold history, emotion, and community in one breath—*ethra scripen vanna*, as the Daughters of Avalon would say: *what is written in resonance, echoes in the soul.*

www.alexanderpaulburton.com

A-Z Of

BEING GAY IN A WORLD WHICH ALSO WANTS TO BE GAY (OR NOT)

BY ALEXANDER PAUL BURTON

#MILLENNIAL TRUTHS

50 Ways to Challenge Antisemitism and Defend Social Justice:

An LGBTQ+ Advocate's Perspective on Law, Society, and Allyship

ALEXANDER PAUL BURTON

CHALLENGING HATE ISN'T JUST A CHOICE;
IT'S A RESPONSIBILITY WE ALL SHARE TO
BUILD A BETTER, KINDER WORLD.

#MILLENNIAL TRUTHS

The Entrepreneurial Odyssey of a Restless Mind

ALEXANDER PAUL BURTON

FOR THE DREAMERS, THE MISFITS, AND
THE ONES WHO REFUSE TO TAKE THE
EASY ROAD

LE VALLON CREUX

ACTE I : LA ROUTE QUI S'ÉCROULE – UNE CHRONIQUE DE MÉMOIRE ET DE BRUME DANS LES DERNIERS JOURS DE ROME

DE ALEXANDER PAUL BURTON

PARTIE 1, ACTE I DU CYCLE DE THARION

THE HOLLOW VALE

THE CRUMBLING ROAD

A CHRONICLE OF MEMORY AND MIST IN THE LAST DAYS OF ROME

BY ALEXANDER PAUL BURTON

PART 1, ACT 1 OF THE THARION CYCLE

#MILLENNIAL TRUTHS

Lost in Translation – A Philosophical Journey Through Japan

翻訳の迷子 –
日本をめぐ
る哲学的旅

ALEXANDER PAUL BURTON

アレクサンダー・ポール・バ
ートン

#MILLENNIAL TRUTHS

Fur, Feathers & Fiascos – The Intellectual's Guide to Pet Ownership (and Surviving It)

ALEXANDER PAUL BURTON

"DOMINI SUMUS IN DOMO NOSTRA, SED SERVIMUS BESTIIS." (WE ARE THE MASTERS OF OUR HOUSE, YET WE SERVE THE BEASTS.)

AN LGBT ARTIST'S
GUIDE TO NAVIGATING
THE INDUSTRY

MARKETING
FOR NEW
MUSICIANS

FROM A WORKING MARKETING PROFESSIONAL

ALEXANDER PAUL BURTON

#MILLENNIAL TRUTHS

A Journey Through
Wit, Woe, and Wi-Fi

ALEXANDER PAUL BURTON

"BY THE TIME YOU UNDERSTAND WHAT LIFE IS
ABOUT, YOU'VE ALREADY PAID OFF HALF YOUR
STUDENT LOANS."